LET'S LEARN ABOUT...
THE SKY

BIG BOOK

K3

TRIXIA VALLE

Pearson Education Limited
KAO Two, KAO Park, Harlow, Essex, CM17 9NA, England
and Associated Companies around the world.

First published 2020

ISBN: 978-1-292-33420-2

Set in Mundo Sans
Printed in China (SWTC/01)

Acknowledgements
The publishers and author(s) would like to thank the following people and
institutions for their feedback and comments during the development of the
material: Marcos Mendonça, Leandra Dias, Viviane Kirmeliene, Rhiannon Ball,
Simara H. Dal'Alba, Mônica Bicalho and GB Editorial.
The publishers would also like to thank all the teachers who contributed to the
develoment of *Let's learn about...*: Adriano de Paula Souza, Aline Ramos Teixeira
Santo, Aline Vitor Rodrigues Pina Pereira, Ana Paula Gomez Montero, Anna
Flávia Feitosa Passos, Camila Jarola, Celiane Junker Silva, Edegar França Junior,
Fabiana Reis Yoshio, Fernanda de Souza Thomaz, Luana da Silva, Michael Iacovino
Luidvinavicius, Munique Dias de Melo, Priscila Rossatti Duval Ferreira Neves,
Sandra Ferito and the schools that took part in Construindo Juntos.

Author Acknowledgements
Trixia Valle

Image Credit(s):
Pearson Education Ltd: Francisco Domínguez 14, 15, 16, Gerardo Sánchez 17, 18,
19, Jaqueline Velázquez 4, 5, 6, Marcela Gómez 7, 8, 9, Mónica Cahué 27, 28, 29,
30, Sheila Cabeza de Vaca 24, 25, 26, Víctor Sandoval 10, 11, 12, 13, Ximena García
Trigos 20, 21, 22, 23

Cover illustration © Filipe Laurentino

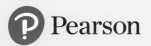

CONTENTS

A COSTUME PARTY

I LIKE MY FACE.

IT IS A ROUND FACE.

I LIKE MYSELF WHEN I SMILE.

I AM SMILING BECAUSE I HAVE A PARTY TODAY.

WE ALL DRESS UP.
I AM A FIREFIGHTER TODAY.
MY HELMET IS RED.
SONIA IS A PIRATE.
SHE HAS LONG, BLACK HAIR.
SHE HAS A PATCH ON ONE EYE.
I CAN'T SEE HER EYE.

LOOK AT THE ELVES!
THEY ARE TOM AND MATT.
THEY ARE TWINS.
TOM IS HAPPY, BUT MATT IS SAD.

WE POP THE BIG BALLOON.
MATT IS NOT SAD. HE'S HAPPY.
WE GET CHOCOLATE AND CANDIES.
WE ARE ALL HAPPY.

MARK'S GLASSES

MARK IS AT HIS SWIMMING LESSON.
EVERYBODY IS LOOKING AT HIS FACE.
THERE IS SOMETHING DIFFERENT.
THE CHILDREN SAY, "HE'S WEARING GLASSES."
MARK LOOKS DOWN. HE WANTS TO GO AWAY.

MR. GORDON ARRIVES. HE LOOKS AT MARK.
MARK IS UNHAPPY.
"WHAT'S WRONG, MARK?" MR. GORDON ASKS.
MARK LOOKS AT THE FLOOR.
HE SAYS, "I CAN'T SEE WITHOUT MY GLASSES.
I CAN'T SWIM WITH MY GLASSES ON."

MR. GORDON SAYS, "DON'T WORRY, MARK.

WE ALL KNOW YOUR EYES ARE IMPORTANT.

HERE ARE YOUR SPECIAL GOGGLES.

YOU CAN SWIM WITH THEM."

ALL THE CHILDREN WANT TO SEE THE SPECIAL GOGGLES.

"COOL," THEY SAY. "YOU CAN SEE BELOW THE WATER!"

MARK IS HAPPY NOW.

HE DIVES INTO THE WATER WITH HIS SPECIAL GOGGLES.

COOKIES FOR GRANDMA AND GRANDPA 04

IT IS GRANDMA AND GRANDPA'S ANNIVERSARY.
THEIR GRANDCHILDREN ARE MAKING COOKIES.
THERE IS FLOUR ON THE TABLE AND THERE'S BUTTER, TOO.
THERE IS MILK. THERE ARE EGGS AND CHOCOLATE CHIPS.

EMMA WANTS TO HAVE SOME FUN. SHE THROWS FLOUR AT HER COUSINS. HER COUSINS THROW FLOUR AT HER.

MOM IS NOT HAPPY. SHE SAYS, "CHILDREN!

WE DON'T PLAY WITH FLOUR!"

THE CHILDREN ARE SORRY. THEY ALL WANT TO SWEEP THE FLOOR AT THE SAME TIME. BUT THERE IS ONLY ONE BROOM.

MOM SAYS, "YOU HAVE TO TAKE TURNS!"

THE KITCHEN IS CLEAN NOW.

THE CHILDREN MAKE THE COOKIES TOGETHER.

THE COOKIES ARE READY TO GO IN THE OVEN.

GRANDMA AND GRANDPA ARE IN THE KITCHEN NOW.

THEY SEE THE COOKIES. THEY ARE SURPRISED.

THEY HUG THE CHILDREN AT THE SAME TIME.

EMMA SAYS, "GRANDMA, GRANDPA! YOU HAVE TO TAKE TURNS!"

EVERYBODY LAUGHS.

A HOLIDAY ON THE BEACH

THE SIMMONS LIVE IN A VERY COLD CITY.

THEY ARE GOING TO THE BEACH FOR A FEW DAYS.

THE CHILDREN ARE VERY EXCITED.

THIS IS THEIR FIRST TIME ON THE BEACH!

ON THE BEACH, DAD SAYS, "WEAR LIGHT CLOTHES."

THEY DON'T LISTEN TO DAD.

THEY ALL RUN TOWARDS THE SEA.

LOOK! SARAH HAS A BIG COAT. MOM HAS BOOTS ON.

KEVIN WEARS JEANS, AND LITTLE BORIS HAS HIS BLANKET.

THEY FEEL REALLY HOT NOW.

THEY ARE SWEATING.

DAD LAUGHS AND SAYS, "WHO WANTS A BATHING SUIT?"

EVERYBODY SHOUTS, "YAY!"

THEY CHANGE THEIR CLOTHES.

THEY ENJOY THE SUN AND THE WARM SEA WATER.

MARTIN HELPS OUR PLANET 🎧 06

WE ARE WATCHING THE CLOUDS.

AND THEN WE SEE A BRIGHT LIGHT, LIKE A STAR.

IT COMES THROUGH THE WINDOW, AND OUR CLASSROOM SHINES.

A STRANGE LITTLE MAN IS IN THE MIDDLE OF THE STAR.

"WOW!" WE ALL SAY.

THE STRANGE MAN SAYS, "HI! I'M MARTIN.
EVERY DAY I FLY ON MY STAR."

"WOW!" WE SAY AGAIN.

"I TAKE CARE OF YOUR PLANET.
LOOK! DON'T WASTE WATER!"

WE SEE THE WATER. WE ARE VERY SORRY.

"YOU HAVE AN IMPORTANT MISSION, CHILDREN.

TAKE CARE OF YOUR PLANET. BYE!"

WE ALL WAVE GOODBYE.

NOW WE TAKE CARE OF OUR PLANET. IT IS OUR HOME.

THE CHOCOLATE FACTORY

THE STUDENTS ARE ON THE BUS. THEY JUMP UP AND DOWN WITH BIG SMILES.

THEY ARE GOING TO THE TEDDY BEAR CHOCOLATE FACTORY. THEY SING AND TALK.

LAURA ASKS FRANK, "WHAT ARE YOU HAVING FOR LUNCH?"

"CHOCOLATE, OF COURSE!" SAYS FRANK. THEY LAUGH.

A NICE LADY WAITS FOR THEM AT THE FACTORY.

SHE SAYS, "GOOD MORNING, CHILDREN!

LET'S VISIT THE FACTORY.

THERE IS ONE RULE: DON'T EAT THE CHOCOLATE!"

THE CHILDREN VISIT THE FACTORY. MMM... IT SMELLS GOOD! THERE IS A LOT OF CHOCOLATE.

FRANK DOESN'T FOLLOW THE RULES. HE EATS MANY CHOCOLATE TEDDIES.

WHEN THE VISIT ENDS, ALL THE CHILDREN GET A BOX OF CHOCOLATE TEDDIES. EVERYBODY IS HAPPY.

THEY SAY THANK YOU AND GOODBYE.

FRANK EATS AND EATS CHOCOLATE ON THE BUS.

WHEN THEY ARRIVE AT SCHOOL, FRANK HAS A STOMACHACHE.

HE FEELS TERRIBLE. HE CRIES.

LAURA AND THEIR TEACHER TAKE FRANK TO SEE THE SCHOOL NURSE.

HE GIVES FRANK SOME MEDICINE. NO MORE CHOCOLATE TODAY!

FRANK SAYS THANK YOU AND PROMISES TO FOLLOW THE RULES.

SUE AND HER FAMILY GO TO THE ZOO.

SUE LIKES THE ZOO!

THERE ARE TIGERS AND PANTHERS.

THERE ARE ELEPHANTS AND GIRAFFES.

THERE ARE MONKEYS AND RACCOONS.

AUNTIE AGATHA GOES TO THE ZOO, TOO.

SHE'S 80 YEARS OLD.

SUE AND LOU HELP AUNTIE AGATHA.

"THANK YOU!" SAYS AUNTIE AGATHA. "I AM HUNGRY!"

"HURRY! HURRY! AUNTIE AGATHA IS HUNGRY!"

THEY ALL GO TO A CAFETERIA.

AUNTIE AGATHA EATS SOME CAKE.

A LITTLE MONKEY WANTS SOME CAKE, TOO.

"STOP!" SAYS SUE. "DON'T FEED THE ANIMALS!"

LOU SAYS, "GO AWAY! CAKE IS NOT GOOD FOR YOU!"

AUNTIE SAYS, "GOOD, SUE AND LOU!

IT'S NICE TO FOLLOW THE RULES."

GAEL LIKES HIS CITY.

HE FEELS HAPPY AT THE PARKS AND ON THE STREETS.

HE NEVER THROWS TRASH ON THE GROUND.

HE LIKES HIS CITY CLEAN.

HIS FAVORITE PLACE IS DOWNTOWN.
THERE IS AN ICE CREAM PLACE DOWNTOWN.
ON FRIDAYS, HIS MOM BUYS ICE CREAM.
HE HAS ICE CREAM WITH HIS SOCCER TEAM.

MARIO IS ANGRY TODAY. THEY LOST THE GAME.
GAEL'S MOM GIVES HIM SOME ICE CREAM TO
MAKE HIM SMILE.

MARIO DOESN'T SMILE. HE EATS HIS ICE CREAM
AND THROWS HIS TRASH ON THE GROUND.

GAEL SAYS, "MARIO, PUT THE TRASH IN THE TRASH CAN!

LET'S TAKE CARE OF OUR CITY. A CLEAN CITY IS A HAPPY CITY."

MARIO IS NOT ANGRY NOW. HE'S SORRY.

HE HELPS PICK UP THE TRASH.

ALL OF HIS FRIENDS HUG HIM. IT'S GOOD TO KNOW WHEN WE MAKE A MISTAKE.

Reading Strategies

Bring as many books as you want to the classroom. Prepare a corner for reading. Have students bring their favorite pillow and allow them to lie down while they "read" or explore a book.

- Before showing the corresponding text to students, present a situation similar to that in the book so students begin thinking about it and relate it to their own experiences and knowledge.

- You can have students work in pairs or small groups to share their ideas with the whole group. They can also imagine a scene and draw it.

- Show the title, subtitle (if there is one), and illustrations on the title page, and ask students to predict what the story will be about. Allow them to speculate and accept all ideas.

- You can show students the text and illustrations and ask if they know anything about the topic.

- Ask one or two questions related to the story, so students listen for the answers or can infer them.

- Once students have become familiarized with the story, ask them to summarize it briefly.

- Put the scenes on construction paper or cardboard, and cut out the pictures of each scene so students can put the story in order. Have students work in pairs for this activity.

Unit 1

A costume party

Activities with students

1. Distribute circles among your students (one red, one yellow, and one green).
2. Help students draw faces in the circles: in the red one, an angry face; in the yellow circle, a sad face; in the green circle, a happy face.
3. These are the "traffic lights" of the emotions.
4. Ask the following and have students show you their feelings using the "traffic lights."

   How do you feel when...

   ... you go to a party?

   ... you drop your ice cream?

   ... you are not allowed to play?

   ... you get birthday gifts?

5. Explain that we all have feelings and when something makes us feel bad, we can feel angry or sad.

Unit 2

Mark's glasses

Activities with students

1. Ask students to tell you five things they can see far away.
2. Tell students to name five things they can see and that are close to them.
3. Blindfold some volunteers and have them walk, holding the shoulder of a classmate, as if they were blind. Be careful with the students.
4. Reflect on how somebody that can't see feels.

Unit 3

Cookies for Grandma and Grandpa

Activities with students

1. Ask students if they have food at their celebrations (birthdays, graduations, etc.).
2. Have them work in groups of three. Ask them how they feel when they do something wrong.
3. Explain how important it is to follow instructions to prevent accidents.
4. Ask them to draw a picture of their face whenever their mom, dad, or caregiver gets upset with them.

Unit 4

A holiday on the beach

Activities with students

1. Have students work in groups of three and describe the weather today.
2. In the same groups, have them say what kind of weather they like. Help them understand that we all like different things.
3. Finally ask them to draw a day that makes them feel angry, happy, or sad.

Unit 5

Martin helps our planet

Activities with students

1. Ask students to work in groups of three, and discuss how they can be careful and not waste water.
2. Have them draw three non-renewable resources (explain what they are).
3. Ask them for some ideas to recycle materials in their classroom.

Unit 6

The chocolate factory

Activities with students

1. In groups of three, have students discuss what would have happened if the boy hadn't eaten so much chocolate.
2. Have them reflect that every action (or choice one makes) has a consequence.
3. Tell students to draw five things that help them stay healthy (e.g. wash their hands, eat vegetables, brush their teeth, exercise, go to bed early, etc.).
4. Make a classroom poster with all their drawings.

Unit 7

At the zoo

Activities with students

1. In groups of three or four, ask students to draw five different animals and what they eat.
2. Have them say why rules are important and why they can't feed the animals in a zoo.
3. Tell them to say what their favorite animal in a zoo is and why.

Unit 8

We love our city

Activities with students

1. Have students draw their flag.
2. Ask them to work in groups of three, and say three ways of taking care of their city or neighborhood.
3. Help them make a box for recycling and keep it in their classroom.